What is Population?

1 · What is Population?

- **Population** is the **number** of people living in a **place**.

2 · Distribution

- **Population distribution** is the spread of **where** people live.

- This can be global, regional or **local**.

3 · Lots of People

Places with **lots** of people, (densely populated), usually have **habitable environments**.

This means they are good to live in:

- flatter land

- good climate with mixture of sun and rain.

Western Europe

Eastern USA

Japan

Why Live There?

Habitable Environment: River Valleys

Areas which are easy to get to and have good resources have larger populations.

River valleys are good places to live because they are:

- sheltered

- have a fresh water supply

- have good transport links

- have good communications.

Examples:

Rhine Valley, Germany

Ganges Valley, India

5 **Habitable Environments: Lowland Plains**

Lowland plains have:

- flat, fertile soil

- good farming land

- good communications.

Examples:

Cereal Farming, East Anglia (UK)

Dairy Farming, Denmark

Why Live There?

6 **Habitable Environments: Good Natural Resources**

Places with lots of natural resources also have lots of people.

The UAE (United Arab Emirates) has lots of:

- fossil fuel (coal, oil, gas)

- materials for industry

- natural ores (iron ore, bauxite).

This makes it a very good place to live.

7 **Habitable Environments: Coastal Plains**

Coastal Plains are highly populated because they have:

- moderate climates

- good trade access

- ports

- tourism.

Examples:

Many ports around Britain

New York, USA

Difficult Places to Live

8   Sparse Populations

- Places with few people (sparse populations) may have **difficult environments**, **climate** or **few resources**.

- Deserts
- Mountains
- Very cold places
- Marshy grounds

9   Adaptation: The Andes

- Small groups of people have **adapted** to live in such places.

- The **Andes, South America**: altitude is high, slopes are steep, soil is poor.

- The people there have used terracing to make the best use of the land.

10   Adaptation: Desert

- The **Bedouin tribes** live in the **Middle East**.

- They move from place to place so they can find food.

- They use camels to move around.

11   World Population

- Although the population of these places is **small**, the **world population is huge** and **still growing** every day.

The Population Explosion

12   World Population

- About **130 million** babies are born each year!

- **Birth Rate** = the number of live babies born per 1,000 people per year.

- **World population** is now almost **7.5 billion** (7,500,000,000!).

13   Death Rate

- About **50 million people** die each year.

- **Death Rate** = the number of people who die, per 1,000 people per year.

14   Growing Fast

- The world population is growing fast.

- The 20th Century (1900s) saw a '**population explosion**'.

Measuring Population

15 Why has the Population Grown?

- **Drop in death rate** led to **rapid growth** in the number of people.

Less people are dying!

But now there are too many people!

16 A Balance

- Population growth depends on **balance** between birth rate and death rate.

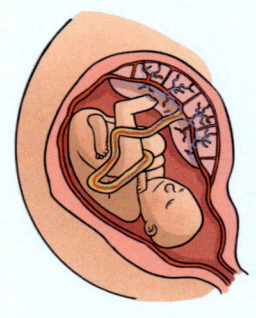 

Birth Rate   **Death Rate**

17 Birth Rate vs Death Rate

- If the birth rate is **higher**, the population **grows (natural increase)**.

 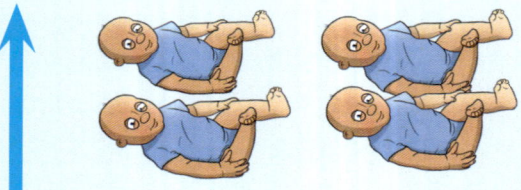

- If the death rate is **higher**, the population **decreases (natural decrease)**.

18 Population Density

- Population Density measures **how many people** live in 1 sq km (average).

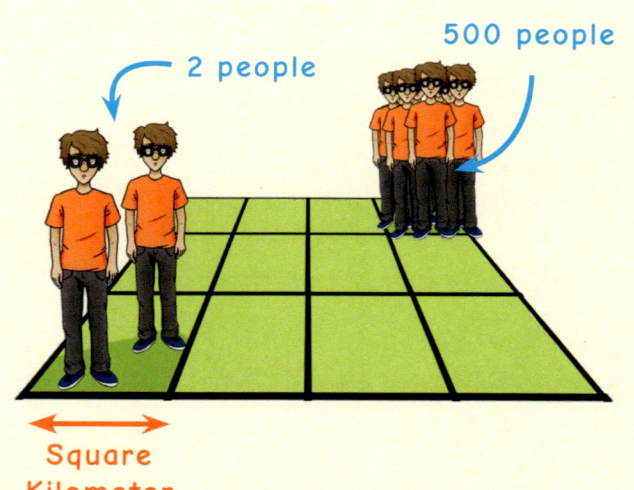

2 people   500 people

Square Kilometer

Population Density

19 Distribution of People

- But, density does **not** show how people are **distributed** in that area (e.g. where they live).

- 1 person may live in 1 street and 300 may live 2 streets away!

20 The Right Number

- We need to have the **right number** of people for the resources.

- This is called **optimum population.**

21 Too Many People

- **Over population** means too many people for the resources in that area.

We have too many people! We will need more resources at this rate.

22 Not Enough People

- **Under population** means there are **too few** people to make use of the resources

We have so many resources! But not many people.

Dense and Sparse Populations

23 | Density Around the World

An area with **high population density** is Bangladesh; 988 people per sq km.

- The UK is 262 per sq km.

- Russia is only 8 per sq km.

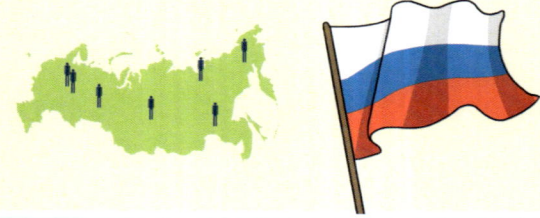

24 | Dense Populations (150+ people per square km)

- **Cities** have **more** people.

- In **London**, there are **5,200 people per sq km.**

25 | Hills + Mountains

- In the **Highlands of Scotland**, there are **10 per sq km.**

- There are steep hills and mountains.

26 | Sparse Populations (0-10 people per sq km)

- The **Pennines and Snowdonia** also have sparse populations.

- These are difficult places to live and work in.

United Kingdom Population

27 UK Cities

In cities, such as Leeds, London, Manchester and Cardiff the population is **dense**.

These cities were **trading places** for wool from the Pennines.

- They grew in the **Industrial Revolution**.
- They are still busy cities with lots of people.

28 Population in the South

- In the **South**, growth has been more recent.
- There are **good transport links** for trade.
- People move to the UK (**migrate**) from Europe.

29 UK & Europe

- The UK has the **3rd highest** population in Europe (**63 million**).

- Germany and France are higher BUT they have much **more** land.

Population Growth Patterns

30 Overcrowding

- In **Dhaka**, capital of Bangladesh, there are **45,000 people** per sq km!

- That is **9 times** as many people as in London!

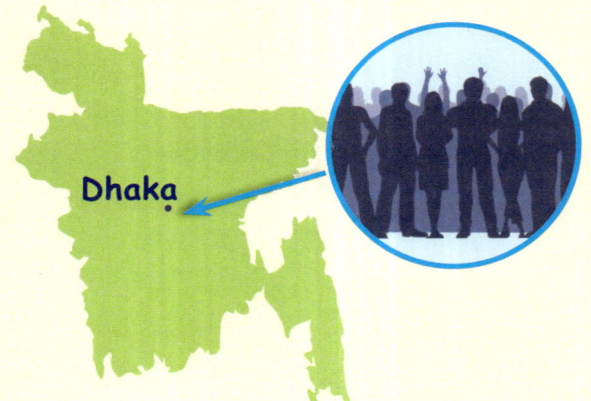

Dhaka

31 Empty Land

- But some areas have **few** people living there.

- So the balance is **not** right.

32 2 Patterns Can Be Seen...

1. All over the World, populations grow **near the coast**.

2. High population is seen in **2 groups of countries**:

- **Developing nations** in Central and East Asia.

- **Developed, wealthy nations** such as Western Europe and North America. (See pages 1 & 2)

North America | Western Europe | Central Asia

developed | developing | East Asia

Population Growth Patterns

33   High Death Rate

- Some **developing** nations have a **high death** rate.
- This is because they do **not** have access to good medical care.

34   High Birth Rate

- But they may also have a **high birth rate** because they do **not have contraception or education.**

35   Migration (my-gray-shun)

- Population may **grow** when people **move into** a country.
- This is a cause of population **increase** in some Western European countries, such as the UK.

Welcome to ENGLAND

36   Fewer Children

- In **developed** countries there is **better medical care** so the death rate has **fallen**.
- But lots of families choose to have **fewer** children.
- So, overall, population growth is slower.

Growth in Population

37 Indonesia

In **developing** countries there has been a **big** population growth:

- Indonesia's population grew from **97 million** (1961) to **260.4 million** in 2016.

- That's a **268%** increase in 54 years.

268% increase in 54 years

38 India

- India; population grew from **361.1** million (1952) to **1.325** billion (2016).

- Increase of **367%** in 64 years!

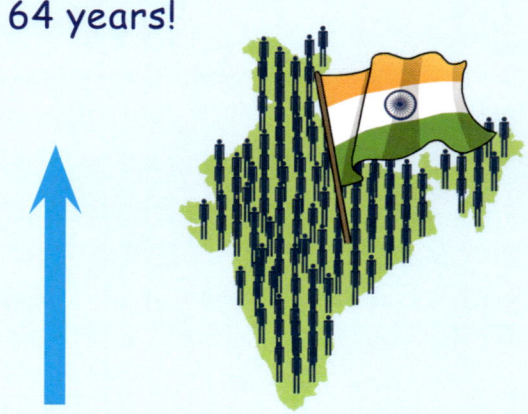

367% increase in 64 years

39 How fast is the population growing?

The United Nations reports:

World population is currently growing at around **74 million** people per year.

74 million per year!

40 More Growth

- Nearly **all** growth is in **less developed** areas. This may rise from 5.3 billion today to 7.8 billion in 2050.

- Population of **more developed** areas will remain **almost the same** (1.2 billion).

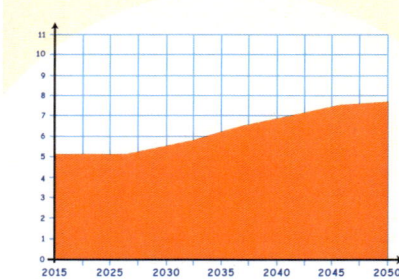

China: 1 Child Policy

41   Over Population

- This growth may lead to **overpopulation**.

If an area does not have enough food, clean water, or shelter, it can lead to **famine** and **malnutrition** (mal-new-tr-i-shun).

42   Control

- Some governments, like China, have taken action to **slow** down population growth.

We must take action to slow population growth!

43   China's '1 child per couple' policy

- China has a '**1 child policy**'.

- There are **good** and **bad** things about this rule.

Only one child per couple!

- This did **control** the **birth rate**, but they will have too many old people.

- Lots of people only wanted **boys**.

- They **ended pregnancies** with girl babies.

- This means there will **not** be enough girls in China in years to come.

The Effect of Growth

   **Demand for Energy**

- **More people** means **more demand** for energy.

- **Developed countries** are increasing the use of **green energy**.

45   **Saving Our Resources**

- NICs (**Newly Industrialised (in-dus-tree-al-iz-d) Countries**) get most power from **fossil fuels**.

- Global demand for energy is bigger than ever.

46   **World Population Growth**

- This graph shows world population growth since 1750.

Key

☐ Developing Countries

☐ Developed Countries

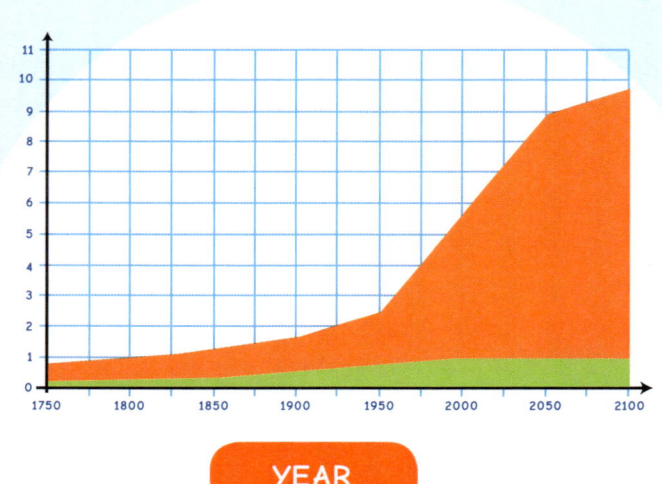

WORLD POPULATION (millions)

YEAR

World Population Map

Persons/Sq Km

2 or less

2 – 10

11 – 40

41 – 500

500 or more

KS3 ONLY: Population Graphs
(Note: You do not need to know these for CE)

47 Population Pyramid (Kenya 2011)

Population pyramids are graphs that show population **structure** (how a population is made up).

- This pyramid for Kenya has **a very wide base.**

- There are a lot of **young** people and people also **die** young.

- This pyramid shape is more likely for a **developing** country where **birth rates** are **higher**.

 Key Male Female

AGE

POPULATION (millions)

48 Population Pyramid (Japan 2011)

The pyramid for Japan is a different shape. It does **not** look like a pyramid.

- The base is not as wide as the Kenyan pyramid.

- The **middle is wide**r and the top is **taller**.

- This type of pyramid is likely to occur in a **developed country.**

- Birth **and** death rates have **fallen**.

AGE

POPULATION (millions)

Key Male Female